Planning

London: H M S O

Researched and written by Reference Services, Central Office of Information.

© Crown copyright 1992
Applications for reproduction should be made to HMSO.
First published 1992

ISBN 0 11 701723 X

HMSO publications are available from:
HMSO Publications Centre
(Mail, fax and telephone orders only)
PO Box 276, London SW8 5DT
Telephone orders 071-873 9090
General enquiries 071-873 0011
(queuing system in operation for both numbers)
Fax orders 071-873 8200
HMSO Bookshops
49 High Holborn, London WC1V 6HB   071-873 0011
Fax 071-873 8200 (counter service only)
258 Broad Street, Birmingham B1 2HE   021-643 3740 Fax 021-643 6510
Southey House, 33 Wine Street, Bristol BS1 2BQ   0272 264306
Fax 0272 294515
9-21 Princess Street, Manchester M60 8AS   061-834 7201 Fax 061-833 0634
16 Arthur Street, Belfast BT1 4GD   0232 238451 Fax 0232 235401
71 Lothian Road, Edinburgh EH3 9AZ   031-228 4181 Fax 031-229 2734
HMSO's Accredited Agents
(see Yellow Pages)
and through good booksellers

Photo Credits

Front cover reproduced from an Ordnance Survey aerial photograph with the permission of the Controller of Her Majesty's Stationery Office © Crown Copyright; cover and centrespread map based upon Ordnance Survey maps used with the permission of the Controller of Her Majesty's Stationery Office © Crown Copyright and London Borough of Wandsworth.

Contents

While every care has been taken in the preparation of this booklet, it does not purport to be a definitive summary or interpretation of planning law.

September 1992

Introduction

Britain[1] has developed a comprehensive system of town and country planning. This aims to secure the most efficient and effective use of land in the public interest, and to ensure that facilities such as roads, schools and sewers are built where they are needed. The system seeks to reconcile the demands for land from industry, commerce, housing, transport, agriculture and recreation, and to protect and enhance the environment by means of a comprehensive statutory system of development control in the public interest. The system provides:

—guidance to help people plan the use of their land confidently and sensibly, and to help planning authorities to interpret the public interest wisely and consistently;

—incentive, in that, by designating land in their development plans for particular types of development, local authorities can stimulate such development; and

—control, which ensures that developers cannot ultimately insist for private reasons on a change that would be against the wider public interest, and that people affected by proposals for change can have their views and interests considered.

Most development requires planning permission from the local planning authority for the area concerned. Planning decisions must be made in accordance with development plans prepared by local

[1]'Britain' is used informally in this booklet to mean the United Kingdom of Great Britain and Northern Ireland. Great Britain comprises England, Scotland and Wales.

authorities, which set out land-use strategies for each area on such matters as housing and industry and development control policies, unless material considerations indicate otherwise. Minor work generally does not require permission. Local planning authorities have powers to deal with breaches of control in their area. In planning law, the term 'development' includes the carrying out of more building, engineering, mining or other operations on land, or making any material change in the use of buildings or land. Demolition is included in building operations.

Overall responsibility for the planning system lies with the Secretaries of State for the Environment, and for Scotland, Wales and Northern Ireland. Responsibility for certain aspects of the system in England, such as the protection of ancient monuments, lies with the Secretary of State for National Heritage. As well as preparing planning legislation and piloting it through Parliament, the Secretaries of State make some decisions on specific matters, such as on 'called-in' planning applications and on appeals against refusal of planning permission by local planning authorities; they also issue guidance to local councils. In Great Britain, local councils have a statutory role as local planning authorities; in Northern Ireland, the Department of the Environment for Northern Ireland handles planning matters through six divisional planning offices, which work closely with the district councils. Public consultation and involvement is an increasingly important facet of Britain's planning system. Essentially, the Government decides which developments require planning permission, and the local planning authorities decide whether to grant it.

This booklet describes the development of Britain's planning system, how it currently operates and how members of the public are involved in the process. It looks at how special areas and buildings of interest are protected and at some of the major issues that are facing the planners.

Government Aims

Government polices on land use planning are set out in the White Paper *This Common Inheritance*, published in September 1990 (see Further Reading, p. 77). Among government commitments are:

—developing government guidance on planning to conserve energy;

—improving the operation of environmental impact assessment;

—encouraging the best location and design of new housing;

—speeding up decision-making for the benefit of the environment and the economy;

—improving the enforcement of planning control; and

—making the preparation of district-wide local plans mandatory and quicker.

This Common Inheritance: the First Year Report, published in September 1991, indicates that significant progress has already been made in achieving these and other planning objectives.

Development of Town and Country Planning

Britain's present system of town and country planning has developed over the course of the twentieth century. Before the system came into being, landowners could largely develop their land as they wished, even if they inconvenienced their neighbours. Some towns or parts of towns in Britain were indeed conceived as a whole—for example Edinburgh New Town, built in the late eighteenth century to a master plan by James Craig (died 1795). In general, however, no control was exercised over urban development and rapid industrialisation brought problems in its wake for the fast-growing areas, due to overcrowding and insanitary conditions. Much earlier attempts to control development had generally proved unsuccessful—for example a decree of Elizabeth I in 1580 which sought to prevent the construction of any new building within three miles of the gates of London, so as to ensure the supply of food and to mitigate the effects of plague. Likewise, Charles II attempted to prevent the rebuilding of London after the Great Fire of 1666 until a new plan for the street layout could be agreed, but was eventually obliged to allow rebuilding on the old sites.

Early Planning Laws

Early attempts were primarily directed at improving standards of drainage, sanitation, ventilation and other similar improvements. The need to improve standards led to nineteenth-century legislation giving local authorities powers to control (by means of local by-laws) such matters as the height of buildings and the width of streets. Several enlightened industrialists built model settlements for their workforces, such as New Lanark and Port Sunlight, designed to provide a better environment than the growing factory towns.

Pressure for the introduction of a proper system of town planning grew with the garden city movement pioneered in the late nineteenth century by Sir Ebenezer Howard (1850–1928). His book *Garden Cities of Tomorrow*, published in 1898, outlined his ideas. Howard wished to 'restore the people to the land' by means of the marriage of town and country. The main aspects of this approach were:

—planned dispersal of industry and people to towns of limited size;

—provision of amenities by way of gardens and parks as well as public buildings;

—a carefully-defined and preserved relationship between town and country;

—pre-planning of the whole town layout and the zoning of the area into town and country areas; and

—unified ownership of all lands in the form of a trust, making it possible to control the use of sites through leases.

All houses were to have gardens as well as easy access to the open country. These ideas led to the founding of two garden cities, Letchworth (1903) and Welwyn (1920), both in Hertfordshire.

Other professional bodies began to call for the introduction of a more general system of planning. The first important piece of planning legislation resulting from such pressure was the Housing, Town Planning Etc. Act 1909. This conferred powers (although not duties) on local councils to prepare town planning schemes with the aims of 'securing proper sanitary conditions, amenity and convenience in connection with the laying-out and use of the land and any neighbouring lands' for any land which was being developed or appeared likely to be developed. The adoption of a scheme under this Act required the approval of central government. Such schemes could indicate the types of development within the areas covered which required the permission of the local authorities; however, there was no general concept of planning permission. Essentially, the scheme constituted a zoning system.

Since there was no duty on local authorities, very few schemes were actually completed under the 1909 Act. After the first world war (1914–18), the Housing and Town Planning Act 1919 attempted to extend the scope of the system by obliging populous boroughs to prepare a scheme; however the original 1926 deadline for doing so was first extended and ultimately abolished. There were a number of other shortcomings in the system as then operated; in particular, landowners could be entitled to compensation if refused permission for development. Since this was very costly to the local authorities, schemes tended to be very broad and hence did not impose great restraint on developers.

Further inter-war planning legislation included the Town and Country Planning Act 1932 and the Restriction of Ribbon Development Act 1935. The 1932 Act extended planning powers to most types of land and provided for a form of interim development control, which operated between an authority resolving to prepare a planning scheme and its final approval by Parliament. In this period, development was allowed to proceed, but once the scheme was approved, the developer could be obliged to remove the development without compensation if it was not in conformity with the scheme.

Development of the Modern Planning System

After the second world war (1939–45), it was decided to address the shortcomings of the system as it then existed. The result was the Town and Country Planning Act 1947, the basis of the present system. This Act:

—entrusted local planning authorities with the duty of preparing development plans for their areas;

—introduced a requirement that any form of development covered by the Act required planning permission;

—introduced enforcement procedures to control breaches of the system;

—allowed local authorities to acquire land compulsorily for planning purposes; and

—appropriated the increased value of the land arising from the grant of planning permission ('development value') to the state, and made provision for landowners to be compensated.

Most of these principles are still part of the planning system today, although the provisions regarding the appropriation of development value were repealed in the early 1950s. Since 1947 there have been various attempts to tax the development value attributable to planning permission. However, that is currently achieved through general taxation, in the form of capital gains tax, and not on a site-specific basis. Because of the growth of new provisions, for example tougher enforcement powers, the main legislation has twice been consolidated, in 1971 and again in 1990. The main legislation at present is contained in the Town and Country Planning Act 1990, although important changes have since been introduced by the Planning and Compensation Act 1991. There were also three complementary consolidating Acts passed in 1990, dealing respectively with hazardous substances, conservation areas and listed buildings, and consequential provisions.

The Planning and Compensation Act 1991 resolved an issue that was causing concern—old permissions for mineral workings granted before the introduction of the present system under the 1947 Act. These old permissions were still valid, and could be invoked at any time; they were restricted by few if any conditions. Indeed, since they predate the planning registers kept by local authorities, the existence of many of them was not known, except to the holder of the permission. Under the new provisions, holders of such permissions had to register them with the appropriate authority by March 1992, or the permission would cease to be valid. Moreover, working on inactive permissions could not commence or recommence until a scheme of operating and land restoration was agreed.

Alongside the primary legislation there is a considerable volume of secondary legislation; of particular importance are the General Development Order (see p. 25) and the Use Classes Order (see p. 28). Also significant is the guidance that the Government has published which, while not having the force of law, must be taken into account in the preparation of development plans and in the determination of planning applications and appeals. There is also a large amount of case law that gives interpretation of the legislation.

Participants in Planning

England and Wales

Central Government

Overall responsibility for the planning system in England lies with the Secretary of State for the Environment. Certain of his functions involve the making of decisions on specific cases; others involve the issuing of guidance to local authorities to assist them in their decision making. His duties and powers with regard to planning include:

— responsibility for new legislation governing the planning system, such as the Planning and Compensation Act 1991;

— responsibility for the Planning Inspectorate, which became an executive agency of the Department of the Environment and the Welsh Office in April 1992;

— issuing guidance on a whole range of policy matters by means of departmental circulars and Planning Policy Guidance notes;

— determining planning applications that he has 'called in' for his own decision (see p. 34);

— deciding appeals against the refusal of planning permission;

— giving strategic or regional guidance to be taken into account by local authorities in drawing up development plans; and

— calling in development plan proposals for approval where his intervention is necessary.

Guidance from the Secretary of State covers a variety of matters. Some of it explains new legislation and advises councils how they should implement it—for example, Department of the Environment circular 16/91 explains the new provisions on planning obligations (see p. 39) introduced by the Planning and Compensation Act 1991. Planning Policy Guidance notes set out broad guidelines on how councils should treat broad policy subjects or particular issues—for example development on unstable land or development which may affect sites of archaeological importance. Guidance does not have the force of law. This is true even for circulars about new pieces of legislation, since the definitive interpretation of legislation is a matter for the courts. However, guidance is a material consideration to be taken into account by local planning authorities in determining planning applications and by the Secretary of State and his inspectors in determining appeals. To ignore it can give rise to awards of costs against planning authorities in appeal cases.

The Secretary of State for National Heritage is responsible for approving the listing of historic buildings and the scheduling of ancient monuments (see p. 54), and for casework decisions in relation to scheduled monuments.

The Secretary of State for Wales has broadly the same powers and duties with regard to Wales. As Wales shares the same legal system with England, legislation on planning usually applies to both. As a result guidance, including circulars, is normally published jointly by the Secretaries of State for the Environment and for Wales. However, where it is appropriate, and to reflect distinct Welsh circumstances, separate guidance is prepared for Welsh local authorities by the Secretary of State for Wales. The Secretary of State has invited the Assembly of Welsh Counties to co-ordinate an assessment of the adequacy of the existing strategic planning framework and to identify the main strategic planning issues likely to affect Wales over a 10-15 year period. This work is being undertaken in collaboration with other interested bodies.

Local Planning Authorities
As local planning authorities, local councils have a number of statutory duties to perform.

Metropolitan districts and London boroughs act as the sole local planning authority for their areas. Their duties and powers include:

—drawing up a unitary development plan (see p. 22) for their area;

—deciding applications for planning permission for new developments and changes of use; and

—taking enforcement action against breaches of planning control.

In non-metropolitan areas, planning responsibilities are split between county councils and district councils. Counties are responsible for drawing up structure plans and local plans covering so-called 'county matters'—principally permission for waste disposal and mineral extraction. They also decide planning applications for county matters. District councils are responsible for drawing up district-wide local plans covering all except county matters, and deciding other planning applications. Parish councils (community councils in Wales) have a statutory right to be consulted on the preparation of local plans and unitary development plans and about planning applications affecting their areas. National Park authorities and the Norfolk and Suffolk Broads Authority (see p. 60) are responsible for carrying out the district roles for their areas, and are also responsible for drawing up policies on county matters within the confines of the Park.

A council with planning responsibilities maintains the services of a planning office, staffed by professional planners and support personnel. The organisation of this is for the council itself to decide, so there is considerable variety. Sometimes, for example, planning is a department in its own right. Other councils might combine it with their economic development division to make one development department. The officers who staff this are responsible for administering the planning system, for example:

—maintaining statutory registers of planning applications and permissions affecting different sites in their area;

—drafting new development plan proposals and organising the associated consultation process;

—meeting applicants to discuss their development proposals and planning applications;

—consulting local residents about proposed developments;

—conducting site visits;

—preparing reports on which the elected councillors base their decisions on individual planning applications;

—deciding certain applications themselves under delegated powers; and

—preparing the council's case in planning appeals and called-in applications.

Officers of other departments might also be consulted about planning applications. For example, if the development could have an effect on traffic, the highways department would be consulted to see if it had any objections—provided that the council was also the highway authority for its area (otherwise it would consult the council which did have highway authority responsibilities). Likewise, for a use that might create a noise nuisance, the environmental health department would be consulted.

The role of the elected councillors is to define the council's planning policies, to take decisions on the more important applications, and to decide whether to take enforcement action on breaches of development control and whether to adopt new development plan proposals. The planning committee is normally the forum where such decisions are taken, although the adoption of a new development plan may be one of the matters reserved in an authority's standing orders to a full meeting of the council.

Councillors will, however, often have a further role in planning matters. Residents concerned about a particular proposal may often consult their ward councillors and ask for their help. This might take the form of speaking for them at a meeting of the planning committee, or perhaps meeting the planning department officers to put concerns to them. Many authorities also allow residents to address the planning committee themselves.

Planning Inspectorate

A Planning Inspectorate has existed for over 80 years to handle planning appeals (see p. 41) and other environmental casework on behalf of the relevant Secretaries of State. The main function of the Inspectorate is the determination of planning appeals in England and Wales, but it also:

—deals with enforcement appeals;

—handles public inquiries into local and unitary development plan proposals; and

—deals with highway orders and other cases, including appeals arising out of applications for discharge consents under the Environmental Protection Act 1990.

In April 1992 the Inspectorate became an executive agency of the Department of the Environment and the Welsh Office, employing some 500 planning inspectors (of whom about half are full-time) and about 400 support and administrative staff. The Government believes that agency status will give the Inspectorate greater responsibility and freedom to use its resources in the most effective manner to achieve the performance targets that have been set for it. Although agency status confers considerable managerial and financial autonomy, the relationship between inspectors and the Secretaries of State in the determination of individual cases remains unchanged.

Public Participation

Public involvement in planning decisions is an important part of the planning system. Local planning authorities should consult the public whenever a development plan is proposed or an existing plan is amended. Once a plan is drafted, people can make comments and formal objections which must be considered. If objections to a local plan are unresolved, there is a public inquiry. Where changes are proposed after a public inquiry, people will again be given the opportunity to make their views known.

Details of all planning applications must be kept by the planning authority in a publicly available register. From May 1992, all planning applications will receive publicity; any member of the public may comment on any application. All comments relevant to the planning issues in the case must be taken into account in determining any planning application.

Other Bodies

Other bodies also have a role to play in planning. These include:

—regional conferences of planning authorities;

—urban development corporations; and

—English Heritage (see below).

Regional conferences of planning authorities have been established in most regions of England so that issues affecting the area of more than one planning authority can be addressed jointly. These conferences play an important part in the Government's consultations before the Secretary of State issues regional planning guidance. For example, one such group is Serplan (the planning conference for south-east England), which publishes a wide range of documents on various matters relating to planning in the South East. These include reports on the regional economy, housing, retailing, transport and waste disposal in the region and draft guidance to the Secretary of State. Within Greater London, the London Planning Advisory Committee (LPAC) was set up to provide draft strategic planning advice after the Greater London Council (GLC) was abolished in 1986. The London boroughs are required to be members of LPAC.

English Heritage (the Historic Buildings and Monuments Commission for England) has important conservation responsibilities. However, in addition to its functions in maintaining historic monuments in the care of the Government and making grants to protect historic buildings, it also has a planning role. It makes recommendations to the Secretary of State for National Heritage, for example with regard to the listing of buildings. In 1990–91 it advised the Government in over 800 applications for scheduled monument consent and was involved in 6,900 listed building consent applications. All major proposals in conservation areas (see p. 52), of which there are some 5,000 a year, must be notified to English Heritage, which can offer advice to the local planning authority concerned. Within Greater London it has wider powers, which were inherited from the GLC on its abolition; all applications for work to listed buildings in London are notified to English Heritage, which is able to direct the boroughs how to deal with them. It also has the power to designate conservation areas in Greater London with the consent of the Secretary of State for National Heritage. English Heritage's powers to prosecute offences under heritage legislation were strengthened by the Planning and Compensation Act 1991. The Welsh heritage body, Cadw, has equivalent functions to English Heritage.

Urban development corporations (UDCs) have been established in 11 inner city areas in order to reverse large-scale urban decline. The first two were established in London Docklands and on Merseyside in 1981. In England, UDCs have taken over development control functions from the relevant local authorities. However, although the UDCs are responsible for deciding planning applications, consultation with the local authorities on planning matters continues, so that elected councillors continue to have some influence over planning in UDC areas. Planning applications within UDC areas are reported to the local council for formal observations. Moreover, since the UDCs have not taken over highway functions, close consultation on traffic matters is needed between the UDC and the highway authority. The preparation of development plans remains the responsibility of the local planning authority, but the UDC must be consulted on development plan proposals.

Scotland

The Secretary of State for Scotland has broadly the same powers as his counterparts in England and Wales. Structure plans are prepared by regional or islands authorities; local plans are prepared by those districts with planning responsibilities and by general planning and islands authorities. The development plan system in Scotland was not affected by the Planning and Compensation Act 1991, which made various changes to the system in England and Wales, although many of the other provisions of the Act do apply to Scotland. The Scottish Office has a small staff of planning inspectors, who deal with the appeal and inquiry work that the Planning Inspectorate handles in England and Wales.

Scotland has a system of 'neighbour notification' of planning applications. This requires the applicant to notify the proprietors of land and buildings adjoining the site of a proposed development at the same time as the application is submitted to the local authority. By contrast, in England and Wales, consultations of neighbours are a matter for the local planning authority, although an applicant has to give notice of an application to anyone with an interest in the land—the owner, for example, or the occupier.

Northern Ireland

Planning in Northern Ireland is the responsibility of the Department of the Environment for Northern Ireland, which maintains six divisional planning offices to handle the workload. Although planning in Northern Ireland is therefore not directly a matter for local authorities, the divisional planning offices do consult with the district councils and work closely with them. Planning appeals can be made to an independent Planning Appeals Commission.

Neighbour notification is carried out by the Department of the Environment, which sends out letters to neighbours from a list of addresses of neighbouring properties as supplied by the applicant. All except minor applications are advertised in the local press.

Development Plans

The relevant local planning authorities are responsible for drawing up development plans, which set out the broad areas in which development is expected and lay down the policies against which applications for planning permission will be judged. There are three main types of development plan in Britain: the structure plan, the local plan and the unitary development plan. Structure and local plans apply to non-metropolitan areas; unitary development plans are being introduced to cover London and metropolitan areas. The development plan system in England and Wales was significantly modified by the Planning and Compensation Act 1991. This introduced:

—a requirement for districts and National Parks to produce district-wide local plans;

—a streamlined system for the adoption of development plans; and

—a presumption that planning decisions will accord with the development plan unless material considerations indicate otherwise.

Structure Plans

In England and Wales, structure plans are drawn up by the county councils after consultation and publicity for the proposals. They consist of a written statement, accompanied by a key diagram, setting out broad land-use policies, and policies for the conservation of natural beauty and amenity, the improvement of the physical environment and traffic management in the area in question. The Lake District and Peak District National Parks are responsible for the structure plans for their areas. Government guidance has summarised the functions of the structure plan as:

—stating the authority's general policies and proposals for the development and use of land;

—taking account of policies at national and regional level as they affect the planning of the area concerned; and

—setting the framework for local plans.

Structure plans should avoid setting out detailed development control policies, as these are contained in local plans.

The sorts of issue that might be addressed in structure plans include:

—housing, including figures for new housing provision in each district;

—Green Belts and conservation of the natural and built environments;

—the urban economy, including major industrial, business, retail and other employment-generating and wealth-creating development;

—strategic transport and highway policies; and

—tourism, leisure and recreation.

Prior to the 1991 Act, structure plans were subject to the approval of the Secretary of State for the Environment and his equivalents. They no longer have to be approved in this fashion, but the Secretary of State retains powers to intervene if necessary. County councils are now responsible for adopting their own structure plan proposals once they have considered objections and held an 'examination in public' in connection with them.

Local Plans

District councils must prepare a local plan for their area; in National Parks, however, the National Park authority is responsible for drawing up a Park-wide plan. Local plans are adopted by the district council or National Park authority concerned, but they must conform generally with the provisions of the structure plan. However, there are reserve powers for the relevant Secretary of State to intervene in plan preparation.

Local plans provide a detailed guide for land-use planning, setting out the council's policies and proposals for the development or other use of land; these are illustrated on a proposals map (see illustrations). A local plan must include policies in respect of:

—conserving the natural beauty and amenity of the land;

—improving the physical environment; and

—managing traffic in the area concerned.

They may also contain proposals for 'action areas'; that is, areas where it is intended that there shall be comprehensive development by public bodies or private enterprise over a comparatively short period of time. As in the preparation of structure plans, there has to be consultation with specified bodies and the public. Objections to local plans are heard by an inspector at a public local inquiry.

The 1991 Act also requires that county councils prepare mineral local plans within the framework of strategic minerals policies in structure plans and, in England, waste local plans. In Wales, policies on waste are to be included in districts' local plans. National Park authorities became responsible for drawing up Park-wide local plans and also took over responsibility for policies for mineral extraction and waste in their areas. These may be the subject of separate plans, be combined with one another or be included in the Park local plans.

Unitary Development Plans

Unitary development plans (UDPs) were introduced following the abolition of the GLC and the metropolitan county councils in 1986. Previously, the GLC and the metropolitan councils had produced structure plans for their areas, while the London boroughs and the metropolitan districts were able to prepare local plans. The new arrangements, originally provided for in the Local Government Act 1985, are for the production of a single UDP. This combines the functions of both plans in a single document. Thus each London borough and metropolitan district must prepare a single mandatory plan covering the whole of its area. Like a local plan, it contains a map showing the authority's proposals for the development and other use of land. Strategic guidance is given by the Government, providing advice on the wider planning issues which the districts and boroughs need to take into account when preparing their UDPs. The provision of such guidance was completed by October 1989.

The new provisions first came into force in a number of London boroughs in August 1989; by July 1990 the provisions were in force in all London boroughs and metropolitan districts. The London Borough of Barnet became the first authority to adopt its UDP in November 1991. Other London and metropolitan authorities are in the process of preparing their UDPs. The public are consulted during the preparation of a UDP and, as with local plans, objections are heard at a public local inquiry.

Regional and Strategic Guidance

Structure and unitary development plans have to take into account regional guidance issued by the Secretary of State. This sets out advice on matters of regional significance, including, for example, the number of new houses that may be required in each county in future years. Guidance notes are updated at regular intervals; for example, revised guidance was published for the South East in 1989, covering the period until 2001. Work is already under way on the replacement guidance, covering the period up to 2006. Guidance has also been published for East Anglia and it is hoped that it will be issued for all regions by the end of 1993.

The various regional planning conferences play an important role in advising the Government before such regional guidances are issued. Before doing so they consult widely with such groups as professional bodies and amenity societies. In general, the Government considers that county councils should have the leading role in advising it on regional matters, but that district councils and National Park authorities should be closely involved. The Secretary of State also publishes strategic planning guidance to provide a framework for the preparation of UDPs in metropolitan boroughs. This guidance has been published for all the former metropolitan counties. The procedure is the same as that for regional planning guidance.

Public Consultation

Public consultation is an important part of the process of formulating and adopting a development plan, or for altering one that is already in force. The procedures vary somewhat between the different types of plans, but in all cases the involvement of the local residents and business interests is seen as important, and considerable efforts are made to secure their comments. Consultation with other authorities is also important, consultation with certain specified bodies being required by regulations.

Various methods are commonly used to consult the public over plan proposals. There may be public displays in libraries and council offices, voluntary groups such as residents' and tenants' associations may be contacted, and advertisements may be placed in local newspapers to alert interested residents. Councils may then amend their draft plans in the light of the comments received. At a later stage, the plan must be placed 'on deposit' for public inspection for a specified period (usually six weeks), which must be advertised locally. Copies are available to be consulted at suitable locations (again, usually libraries and council offices) and members of the public can make formal objections. There is a right for objections duly made to a local plan (including waste and minerals local plans) or to a UDP to be heard at a public local inquiry.

Development Control

Development control is the process by which local planning authorities ensure that new buildings, changes of use or alteration of existing buildings in their areas are acceptable. Most forms of development require the consent of the relevant local planning authority; this is generally known as 'planning permission'. Applications are decided by the local planning authority on the merits of each individual case in the light of development plans and other material considerations.

Requirements for Planning Permission

Not all forms of development need a specific planning permission. The boundaries of control are generally laid down by the Government. The General Development Order sets out a whole range of provisions relating to the operation of the system and the grant of planning permission. It sets out 'permitted development' rights enabling development of a variety of types to be carried out without the need for a specific planning application. This category includes such works as:

—loft conversions and dormer windows;

—small extensions, provided that certain requirements are fulfilled;

—garages and outhouses, again with certain restrictions;

—porches, provided they are not too large or too close to the roadway;

—hedges and low fences;

—television aerials; and

—one small satellite dish per dwelling, provided it is below the roofline.

Planning applications do, however, have to be made for a large number of purposes. These include:

—the construction of all significant buildings;

—extensions which would add more than 15 per cent to the volume of the building;

—most garages which are situated closer to the road than the original house;

—some works which would affect a listed building;

—change of use from one category to another (see p. 27); and

—the display of certain advertisements and signs.

Furthermore, the local planning authority can restrict permitted development rights in defined areas by means of an 'article 4 direction' (see p. 53). People living in specially protected areas such as a conservation area or National Park are also more restricted in what they can do without planning permission.

Certain types of work are not classed as development. Until recently, for example, there was no control over the demolition of houses (other than listed buildings or those in conservation areas), since demolition was not regarded as development. The Planning and Compensation Act 1991 brought demolition within the scope of the planning system. In most circumstances, however, demolition now counts as permitted development. Local planning authorities are able to make use of an article 4 direction to remove this permitted development right in a particular case or in a vulnerable area. The owner would then have to apply for planning permission to be allowed to proceed with the demolition.

Agricultural buildings have in the past enjoyed very wide scope for permitted development; although tighter regulations have now been introduced (see p. 59), farming developments are still treated somewhat differently. Other exemptions from normal planning procedures are provided by the presence of enterprise zones and simplified planning zones (see p. 51).

Planning permission is said to 'run with the land'. In other words, it passes to anyone who buys the land. Indeed, it is not necessary for someone actually to own a piece of land before applying for planning permission. However, once permission has been granted, the applicant would then have to buy the land or otherwise get the owner's consent before carrying out any development; failure to do so would be a trespass that could be dealt with in the civil courts. Councils do, however, sometimes apply a condition that planning permission (usually for a change of use) shall be personal to the applicant. This means that if someone else takes over the property, it reverts to its former use.

Changes of Use

Some of the different uses to which a building or piece of land can be put are categorised under the Use Classes Order, which applies to England and Wales. Various categories and sub-categories are given, and planning permission is generally needed to change from one use to another. No permission is needed to change use within a class. The use of a building will generally be either what it was built as, what it was used for in 1948 (the date when the 1947 Act came into force) or a use granted by a planning permission. A change of use only covers the use of a building or piece of land; it does not cover any physical alterations to the building that may be needed to equip it for the new use. Generally planning permission would be required for this work.

Until recently, landowners could apply for a 'certificate of established use' if a use of land had begun before 1964 and had continued without any material change. This gave the owner immunity from enforcement action, but does not make the use lawful. Under the Planning and Compensation Act 1991, a new system of 'certificates of lawful use' was introduced in July 1992. This means that if the use is changed unlawfully and not enforced, then after ten years the owner will be able to apply for a lawful use certificate.

The Use Classes Order

The Use Classes Order provides a classification of uses:

A1   *Shops*—sale of goods other than hot food, and services such as hairdressing and dry cleaning to visiting members of the public.

A2   *Financial and Professional Services*—services provided principally to visiting members of the public, including financial services and betting offices.

A3   *Food and Drink*—such as pubs, restaurants and sale of hot takeaway food.

B1   *Business*

B2   *General Industrial*

B4–B7 *Special Industrial Groups B–E*—certain specialised (generally 'bad neighbour') industrial uses such as smelting, distilling oils, and rendering animals.

B8   *Storage or Distribution*

C1   *Hotels and Hostels*—a residential institution where no significant element of care is provided.

C2   *Residential Institutions*—hospitals, nursing homes, boarding schools, residential accommodation for people in need of care.

C3   *Dwelling-houses*

D1   *Non-residential Institutions*—for example, health services, schools, museums, libraries and places of worship.

D2   *Assembly and Leisure*—such as cinemas, concert or dance halls or sports facilities.

There are also the so-called '*sui generis*' uses, which fall outside the provisions of the order. These include theatres, amusement arcades, launderettes, car sales and taxi businesses. Changes to or between these uses require planning permission if they amount to a material change of use.

Applications

Application Fees

Applications for planning permission are made to the local planning authority. Outside metropolitan areas, applications are made to the district council, except for applications for county matters which go directly to the county council. The applicant has to supply information about what is proposed, for example by submitting architect's drawings, and has to pay a fee to the authority. The level of fee is set by the Government and varies according to the size of the proposed development.

Table 1: Examples of Application Fees
with effect from 2 January 1992

	£
Erection of a dwelling-house	110
Extension of a dwelling-house	55
Change of use	110
Permission to display a shop name	30
Outline planning applications,	
per 0.1 hectare of a site	110
Erection of non-residential buildings,	
per 75 square metres of floor space	110
up to a maximum of	5,520

Processing Applications

Applications can either be in detail or in outline. An outline permission establishes the principle of a particular development on a site, and is then followed by a further application once the detailed design has been worked up. Developers may, however, apply for full permission without going through the outline stage.

Once submitted, most applications should be dealt with within eight weeks, or 16 weeks if environmental assessment (see p. 33) is needed. If the local planning authority does not give a decision within this period and has not agreed an extension, the applicant is entitled to appeal to the Department of the Environment or its counterparts in Wales, Scotland and Northern Ireland on the ground of non-determination. Therefore some developers of large projects may submit two identical applications. An appeal is then made on one of them after the eight-week period has elapsed. This 'twin-tracking' procedure was previously assisted by a 75 per cent

rebate on the fee for the second application; however, this conces-
sion was removed in January 1992.

Table 2: Planning Applications and Decisions, England

thousands

	Applications received	Applications decided	Applications granted
1981–82	372	407	349
1982–83	411	382	334
1983–84	430	404	354
1984–85	421	399	345
1985–86[a]	432	402	344
1986–87	534	493	406
1987–88	598	542	446
1988–89	683	620	498
1989–90	628	596	464
1990–91	532	518	401
1991–92	510	483	381

Source: Department of the Environment.

[a] Break in series after 1985-86; before that time, the statistics do not include such applications as advertisement consent, listed building consent and established use certificates.

The number of applications has declined in recent years; this coin-
cides with the recent weakness in the property market. Conversely,
during the property boom of the late 1980s, the number of applications reached a very high figure. About 60% of the applications
were decided within the eight-week period, although councils vary
considerably in their performance in meeting this target. In
London, for example, in 1990–91 one borough decided 68 per cent

of applications inside eight weeks, while another only dealt with 15 per cent. The Government encourages councils to improve their performance in considering applications within time.

Would-be developers often engage in informal discussions with the planning officers both before they put in an application and also once the application has been submitted. This enables them to obtain further indications, beyond what is available in development plans, as to whether the council is likely to look favourably on the proposal or application. Also, if the council officers have reservations about particular aspects of an application, developers have the chance to find this out at an early stage and to see if there are ways to overcome the objection. Amended drawings are often submitted to deal with the planning authority's reservations about particular aspects of the development.

Once an appeal has been made, however, the local planning authority no longer has the power to decide an application; it has to be determined by the Secretary of State or one of his inspectors.

Public Consultations

Local residents are involved in the development control process by the consultations carried out by the local planning authority. A public register of applications must be maintained and made available for inspection. Moreover, councils are obliged to advertise all applications, so as to give the public an opportunity to comment. Methods of publicising applications can include placing advertisements in local newspapers, putting up notices on the site or informing neighbours directly.

Many authorities consult even more widely than they are obliged to by law, in order to ensure public involvement in the planning process. People directly affected are often contacted by letters sent out by the council's planning department—about three-quarters of local planning authorities in England and Wales do this. Interested bodies, such as residents' associations, often make a point of obtaining the list of planning applications in their areas, so that they can make representations on schemes that affect their locality.

Those who wish to comment on a scheme can write to the planning department, setting out their views. Often, objectors will lobby councillors sitting on the planning committee and organise and submit petitions. Councillors who do not sit on the planning committee may also become involved in local planning issues at the request of their electors, often attending the planning committee meeting to argue a case on behalf of objectors.

In addition, where a development is proposed close to the boundary of one local planning authority with another, so that the area of the other local planning authority might be affected, the authority dealing with the application has to consult with the other one, and ask it to make 'formal observations'.

Despite the provisions for publicity, many people felt that insufficient consultation took place, and a large number of complaints to the local government ombudsman concerned alleged failure to publicise applications. The Government therefore introduced a requirement for all planning applications to receive publicity from July 1992.

Environmental Assessment
Consideration of the environmental effects that a particular development would have on the area has for a long time been part of the planning process. However, as the result of a European Community directive which came into force in 1988, special envi-

ronmental assessment procedures now apply to some proposals. The directive requires that consent shall not be given for certain types of major development likely to have significant environmental effects before those effects have been considered. In such cases the would-be developer must prepare and submit with the planning application an environmental statement setting out the developer's own assessment of the likely environmental effects of the proposal. Consultation with the authorities charged with environmental responsibilities and with the public is an important part of the process and their views must be taken into account by the local planning authority when deciding the application.

Determination of Applications

Normally, an application is decided by the relevant local planning authority. However, the Secretary of State may 'call in' an application to determine it himself. This power is used sparingly. Applications which have more than local interest are sometimes called in. Also, where a council proposes to grant an application for development involving a substantial departure from the provisions of a local plan, it must inform the Secretary of State so that he can consider whether to call in the application. The Secretary of State also has the power to order a council not to decide an application until he has had time to consider calling it in. For example, in February 1992 the Secretary of State decided to call in two applications relating to the redevelopment of Paternoster Square adjacent to St Paul's Cathedral in the City of London. This was because of the national importance of the site and the need to ensure that it was developed in a coherent way and to high standards. He had previously directed that the City Corporation should not decide these applications until he had had time to consider whether or not to call them in.

Most applications are determined by local planning authorities. They are decided in one of two ways. An application may be decided by the elected councillors, usually meeting in a planning committee. However, because councillors serve in a voluntary capacity and are often available to meet only in the evenings, it is often convenient to have the full-time officers decide certain applications under delegated powers. These will normally be routine and uncontroversial applications. A scheme of delegation usually sets out which applications can be decided by officers and which must go before the councillors. Whether an application is dealt with by officers or by the elected councillors, the same basic procedures have to be followed.

A typical scheme of delegation might specify that all applications are to be decided by the council officers, except:

—those recommended for approval contrary to the provisions of the approved development plan;

—those which are controversial or raise major issues of a planning nature; or

—those requested to go to the committee by the councillors for the ward in question.

If an application is decided by the councillors at the planning committee, this will be a meeting open to the public. Exceptionally, if confidential or exempt business—as defined by the Local Government Act 1972—is to be discussed, the councillors can agree to meet in closed session. Agendas and reports from officers are likewise public documents and must be made available for inspection at the council offices three working days in advance of the meeting, except in cases of urgent matters. Objectors and supporters of particular development proposals will often therefore take the opportunity to turn up in person to show the strength of their feelings, and they may be allowed an opportunity to speak and put their case. Their written representations, together with any other relevant considerations, would be put before the councillors in a report compiled by the planning officers. This would typically:

—set out the nature of the application, any relevant planning history of the site, and the results of public consultation;

—assess the proposals against the development plan policies relevant in the particular case; and

—provide councillors with a recommended course of action.

A typical format for a planning committee deciding an application might be as follows:

—the applicant addresses the committee and councillors ask questions;

—objectors address the committee and councillors ask questions;

—officers introduce their report on the application and councillors ask questions;

—the councillors discuss the matter and one of them moves a proposal;

—councillors may move amendments;

—councillors vote first on any amendments and then on the main motion.

Each application has to be treated on its merits, and irrelevant considerations cannot be taken into account; the council must look solely at the planning grounds for accepting or rejecting the application. Until the Planning and Compensation Act 1991, there was a general presumption that an application would be granted unless there was a clear planning reason for turning it down. The 1991 Act requires that all applications are determined in accordance with the development plans unless material considerations indicate otherwise.

When making its decision, the council can only take into consideration legitimate planning matters. The grounds on which a council can refuse an application are more limited than is often realised. The planning system does not usually address questions of need for a particular activity or use in an area. Thus, for example, local residents may object to a proposal for a change of use of a building to a snooker hall, perhaps because they fear disturbance to the neighbourhood, and add as a reason for the council to reject the application that there are already enough snooker halls in the area. This latter point is not a planning consideration, and the council could not take such arguments into account. The proprietor might well be taking a commercial risk in opening in an area already well-served by similar facilities, but that is not a matter for the planning system to address.

Likewise, the Government advises that, in general, local planning authorities should avoid imposing their own views about the appearance of a proposed building, although occasionally on prominent sites permission might be refused for a building that was considered very undistinguished architecturally.

Once the councillors have voted to approve an application or it has been agreed by officers under delegated powers, that does not mean that it has actually received planning permission. The planning permission is technically only granted when the local planning authority sends the applicant a 'decision letter' setting out the grant of the permission and any conditions that have been attached to it. Usually, this is a formality, but there may be matters that remain to be agreed between the council and the developer, especially if the councillors have approved the application subject to the making of a planning obligation. In such cases, it may after all prove not possible for both sides to agree, and as a result planning permission might not be granted.

If an application is refused, again a decision letter must be sent to the applicant. This must set out the grounds on which this refusal has taken place. Where an application is refused, the applicant has the right to appeal to the relevant Secretary of State—in England the Secretary of State for the Environment.

Conditions

A local planning authority is able to grant an application subject to conditions. A very wide range of conditions is possible. These may govern such matters as the operation of the new development once it is built or to what is done on site before construction commences, but should only be imposed where they are necessary, reasonable, enforceable, precise and relevant both to planning and the development to be permitted. Matters that conditions may relate to include:

—the hours of operation of premises once the development is complete;

—means of restricting nuisance, such as the fitting of noise insulation and fume extractors in premises such as restaurants and wine bars;

—archaeological excavations prior to building work on sites thought likely to be of historic interest;

—landscaping and planting the grounds of the completed building;

—that the building must be made accessible to disabled people;

—that permission is personal to the applicants only, so that their successors must apply again to continue that use; and

—that restaurants must serve only eat-in meals and not provide takeaways (sometimes used in a location where users of a take-away restaurant would cause a traffic hazard).

One standard condition is that development must be commenced within five years of the planning permission being granted; this is a requirement of the Town and Country Planning Act 1990. If the development is not started within this timespan, the permission lapses and the developers would have to apply again if they still wished to proceed with their proposal.

The local planning authority must give the applicant the reasons for imposing conditions. If the applicant does not agree with the imposition of a particular condition, he can appeal, just as if the application had been refused.

Planning Obligations

'Planning obligations' may consist either of a legal agreement between a developer and the local planning authority, or of a one-sided undertaking entered into by the applicant. They should be entered into only in circumstances where the benefit sought is related to the development and is necessary to the grant of permission. Like planning permission, such obligations run with the land and can be enforced against any successor of the original developer; however, a developer must have a legal interest in the land concerned before entering into a planning obligation.

Councils have the right to enter into legal agreements with an applicant for the purpose of regulating the development. These are often known as 'section 106 agreements', after the section of the

1990 Act which authorises them. Although agreements can contain many different provisions, one such is for the developer to agree to pay some money to the local planning authority in order to fund some work connected with the development. For example, if the presence of a new shopping complex is likely to put pressure on the local roads, the developer may agree to pay for the cost of an appropriate traffic scheme. The funding of community benefits is also often established under this section; for example the developer may agree to provide a public park on part of the site. The Government gives local authorities guidance on the use of such agreements, listing the conditions under which it may be suitable to make an agreement. This stresses that an unacceptable development should not be accepted because of the benefits offered, nor should an acceptable development be refused because the developer is unwilling to offer benefits.

The Planning and Compensation Act 1991 introduced the concept of planning undertakings—a one-sided undertaking that the developer can enter into. This is intended for use in cases where the developer believes that a legal agreement might be suitable to resolve objections to a scheme but where the local planning authority is unwilling to enter into one, or where negotiations are too protracted or unreasonable demands are being made. Such an undertaking can be enforced against the developer in the courts in the same way as an agreement with the local planning authority.

Appeals

If a planning application is turned down by a local planning authority, the would-be developer can appeal against this decision to the
relevant Secretary of State. There is also a right of appeal against
the imposition of conditions. If the council fails to decide on the
application within eight weeks, the applicant can again appeal
against 'non-determination'.

The right of appeal is limited to applicants, and does not
extend to any third party. Prior to the establishment of the planning system, a landowner had very wide rights to do as he pleased
with his land, and his neighbours had few rights to prevent him
putting up new buildings even if this harmed their amenity. The
introduction of planning legislation restricted the right of the
landowner to do as he pleased; the local planning authority was able
to prevent many possible developments. The appeals procedure
therefore provides a measure of protection against councils being
over-restrictive on development (another is the purchase notice
procedure—see p. 44).

Objectors do, however, count as 'interested parties' and may
make submissions in the appeal process. They sometimes take part
in, or are represented at, public inquiries, although they may
decide against this and leave the local planning authority to defend
the original refusal of planning permission. It is also possible for
objectors to challenge the actions of a council in the High Court, for
example by seeking a judicial review. Court challenges can also be
made over appeal decisions—there were 143 such challenges in
1990-91. However, most of these were made not by objectors but
by appellants whose appeals had been refused by the Inspectorate.

Generally, each party in an appeal meets its own costs in preparing and presenting its case. However, if the inspector finds that one side or the other has been unreasonable in its conduct, for example by refusing permission without good grounds or by appealing against a well-founded refusal and has thereby caused the other party to incur unnecessary expenditure, an order can be made for the side acting unreasonably to pay the costs of the other party.

Table 3: Appeals against Refusal and Non-determination England and Wales

	Appeals received	Appeals decided	Appeals allowed
1986–87	20,886	15,613	6,534
1987–88	23,548	19,342	7,236
1988–89	29,892	22,035	8,058
1989–90	33,987	27,912	9,281
1990–91	28,409	27,835	9,359

Methods of Dealing with Planning Appeals

There are three ways in which an appeal can be handled. The first and most commonly used is the 'written representations' procedure; the others are by means of a public local inquiry or an informal hearing in front of an inspector. The appellant and the local planning authority may specify which they wish to follow. Most appeals are decided by written representations; of over 26,000 cases decided in England in 1990-91, more than 23,000 followed the written representations procedure.

The vast majority of planning appeals are decided directly by inspectors, while matters of more importance are 'recovered' for

Where publicity has to be given to a planning application, it can be done in various ways. Here, a site notice from Southwark Council lets local people know of proposed alterations to a house in a conservation area.

Planning officers from Epsom and Ewell District Council discuss an application for planning permission for a new supermarket. As well as site plans and architects' drawings, such matters as samples of the brickwork to be used are examined (*left*).

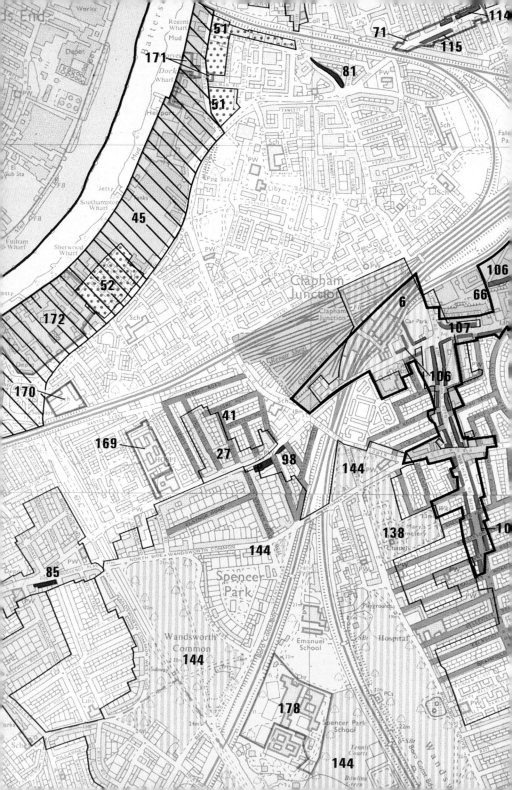

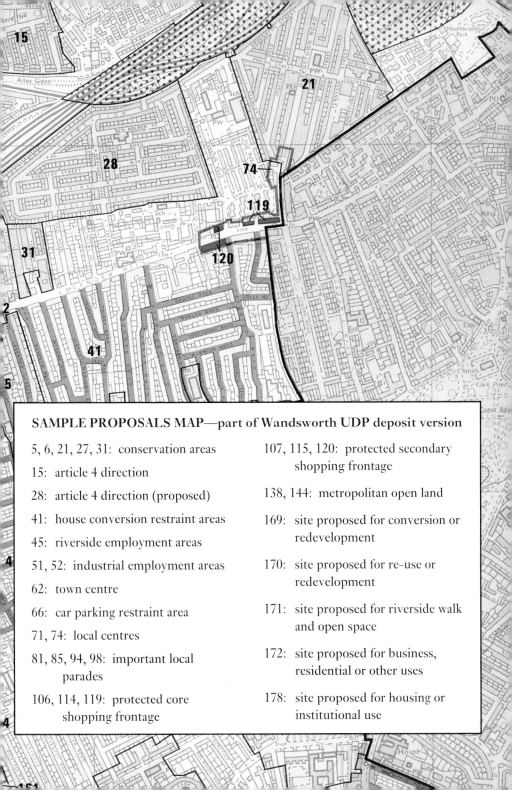

SAMPLE PROPOSALS MAP—part of Wandsworth UDP deposit version

5, 6, 21, 27, 31: conservation areas

15: article 4 direction

28: article 4 direction (proposed)

41: house conversion restraint areas

45: riverside employment areas

51, 52: industrial employment areas

62: town centre

66: car parking restraint area

71, 74: local centres

81, 85, 94, 98: important local parades

106, 114, 119: protected core shopping frontage

107, 115, 120: protected secondary shopping frontage

138, 144: metropolitan open land

169: site proposed for conversion or redevelopment

170: site proposed for re-use or redevelopment

171: site proposed for riverside walk and open space

172: site proposed for business, residential or other uses

178: site proposed for housing or institutional use

By designating conservation areas, local authorities can seek to preserve and enhance the special character of parts of their area. This attractive terrace in south-east London comes under the special protection of the Camberwell conservation area.

As with conservation areas, stringent planning controls exist in National Parks. Here two ramblers enjoy the natural beauty of Loughrigg Fell, near Ambleside, Cumbria, in the Lake District National Park.

decision by the Secretary of State. Appeals that are recovered in this way include:

—residential developments of more than 150 homes;

—retail proposals of more than 100,000 sq ft;

—cases giving rise to significant public controversy, legal difficulties or novel issues of development control;

—proposals for significant development in the Green Belt (see p. 56);

—proposals to which other government departments have objected;

—major minerals proposals; and

—appeals which can only be decided in conjunction with another case over which the inspectors have no jurisdiction.

In the above cases, the inspector makes recommendations, which the Secretary of State may accept or reject.

Written Representations

The written representations method is the simplest and hence generally the cheapest of the procedures. The appellant submits his case in writing, and the council then also submits its case, again in writing. Interested parties may also make their views known in writing. The inspector conducts a site visit and then determines the appeal on the basis of the written submissions, or makes a recommendation to the Secretary of State if the appeal is 'recovered' for his determination.

Public Local Inquiries

Alternatively, the case may be presented in person to the inspector at a formal public local inquiry. It is common for barristers or solicitors to be hired to present the cases on behalf of the appellant, the council and, more rarely, other possibly 'interested parties'—for example, nearby residents who have objected to the proposal. Since this is expensive, however, appellants often use other professionals and objectors may appear in person. After hearing the evidence, the inspector decides the case and gives a decision in writing to the parties or, if the inquiry was held on an application that was being determined by the Secretary of State, makes recommendations to him. The Secretary of State is, however, free to decide the appeal contrary to the inspector's recommendations if he wishes (although in the great majority of cases he follows the inspector's recommendations).

Hearings

Where either of the principal parties wishes to be heard, a 'hearing' may be offered to them instead of a local inquiry, if the appeal appears to be suitable for the more informal procedure. The hearing procedure involves a discussion led by the inspector, and is designed to create a more relaxed atmosphere than a formal inquiry. The procedure is regulated by a code of practice rather than statutory rules. It is suitable for the more straightforward and less controversial transferred appeals, where cross-examination is not required and there are few or no local objectors. Hearings have become increasingly popular with unrepresented appellants, and the number of hearings each year has grown recently to over 1,000.

Purchase Notices

The purchase notice procedure is another safeguard against councils being too restrictive in their planning decisions. If, as a result of a planning decision, a particular site becomes incapable of beneficial use, the owner can serve the council with a notice to purchase it, subject to certain conditions. The notice is subject to confirmation by the Secretary of State and, if upheld, the council is then obliged to buy the land at the price it would have fetched but for that decision.

Enforcement

The refusal of planning permission for a particular development or change of use does not of itself stop the applicant from going ahead regardless. Likewise, people sometimes carry out developments without realising they need planning permission. It is therefore necessary to have means of enforcing planning control.

It is not in itself an offence to carry out a development without planning permission; it is merely unlawful, and the person committing the breach cannot be punished for it. Councils would normally seek to proceed in co-operation with the developer to regularise the situation if this was reasonable. Thus, for example, if planning permission has not been sought, but the development was generally felt to be acceptable by the authority, its officers would invite the developer to submit a retrospective application. This would be dealt with in the same way as if the development had not been started, and if permission is duly granted, then the breach of planning control will have been regularised.

Enforcement Notices

In some cases however, it is necessary to take stronger action, and one way for the local planning authority to proceed is to issue an 'enforcement notice'. This may be served where there has been development without planning permission, or where conditions attached to a planning permission have not been complied with.

This notice is served on the contravener and other people with a legal interest in the land. It must set out the way in which planning control has been breached and any steps which the local planning authority requires to be taken to remedy the breach. The notice cannot come into force until at least 28 days after it has been served; within this period the recipient of the notice may appeal to the Secretary of State. If there is an appeal, the coming into force of the notice is delayed until after the appeal has been decided. If there is no appeal, or if the appeal upholds the notice, the notice takes effect. The breach of planning control then becomes a prosecutable offence. The maximum fine in a magistrate's court for this, previously £2,000, became £20,000 in January 1992 for offences committed since that date.

In general, it is necessary to take action within four years of a breach. Thus, if a development takes place without permission but is not noticed by the local planning authority for at least four years, then enforcement action cannot be taken if the breach later comes to light.

In 1990–91, some 67 per cent of enforcement notices appealed against were upheld by the Inspectorate. In 30 per cent of cases the notice was quashed, while the remaining 3 per cent of notices were varied by the inspector but were otherwise upheld.

Stop Notices

A further legal device that local planning authorities can use to remedy planning breaches is the 'stop notice'. This can be used for dealing with breaches of planning control that require urgent action, since the enforcement notice procedure can take a very considerable time to become effective.

Stop notices are closely linked to enforcement notices, in that a stop notice can only be issued where an enforcement notice has also been served. The stop notice takes effect virtually at once, and cannot be appealed against. However, if the linked enforcement notice is quashed on appeal, the stop notice is also void. If the stop notice is overturned, even on technical grounds, the local planning authority may be liable to pay compensation for loss of profits. Therefore councils tend to be circumspect in their use of stop notices, and use them only in cases of great urgency.

New Enforcement Powers

Following concern that the existing enforcement system was insufficiently powerful, the Government set up an inquiry chaired by Robert Carnwath QC. This produced its conclusions in 1989, *Enforcing Planning Control*, known as the Carnwath Report (see Further Reading). This made several recommendations, including:

—the introduction of breach of condition notices and contravention notices;

—a procedure to legitimise changes of use after ten years; and

—a more rational procedure to determine the lawful use of land.

As a result of the Government accepting the Report's conclusions, the Planning and Compensation Act 1991 gives local planning authorities increased powers to enforce planning decisions, including greater penalties. The Act's provisions include two additional means of proceeding: the breach of condition notice and the planning contravention notice. The Act also implemented other recommendations of the Carnwath Report, including the introduction of lawful-use certificates.

Planning Contravention Notices

This gives local planning authorities the power to obtain information about activities on land where a breach of planning control is suspected. It includes provisions for an owner's or occupier's representations to be considered by the authority. Failure to comply with such a notice within 21 days is an offence and can be punished in the magistrates' court. The planning contravention notice procedure came into force in July 1992.

Breach of Condition Notices

This procedure enables a local planning authority to take action against a breach of a planning condition by serving a notice requiring compliance with the condition. Failure to comply within the time-limit is again an offence. The breach of condition notice procedure also came into force in July 1992.

Other Provisions

The Act's other enforcement provisions include:

—the power for a local planning authority to seek a court injunction against an actual or threatened breach of planning control;

—a new ten-year limit for enforcement action against most unauthorised material changes of use or breach of conditions; and

—improved enforcement notice and stop notice procedures, including the application of stop notices to residential caravan sites.

Planning Compensation

Planning compensation is payable in certain circumstances where existing planning permission to carry out development is withdrawn or restricted. Normally, such compensation is payable by the local planning authority under the provisions of the Town and Country Planning Act 1990, as amended by the Planning and

Compensation Act 1991. The purpose of such an entitlement is to protect the interests of people who may have incurred expenditure relying upon an existing planning consent and had undertaken development which was subsequently subject to an adverse decision by an authority.

When an application for planning permission is made in the usual way to a local planning authority, refusal or restriction of consent does not carry any statutory entitlement to compensation.

Special Cases

There are a number of special cases where the normal rules and procedures of the planning system are modified or policy is applied differently, to cater for a wide variety of situations, varying from inner city areas in need of regeneration to historic buildings and monuments which it is recognised should be protected.

Enterprise Zones and Simplified Planning Zones

Enterprise zones were first introduced by the Government in 1981 as an urban regeneration measure; a total of 27 have been created in many different parts of Britain. Once declared, an enterprise zone lasts for ten years; the early enterprise zones have therefore reached the end of their life. Enterprise zones provide a variety of benefits for businesses that locate in them, including exemption from non-domestic rates and favourable tax allowances on investment. However, there is also a special simplified planning regime for such areas. Under this, a general permission is given for any development in the enterprise zone, except for those specified in the order establishing the zone, or for any class of development specified in the order.

Simplified planning zones (SPZs) were provided for in the Housing and Planning Act 1986, which came into force in the autumn of 1987. By April 1991, six schemes had been adopted and nine more were being seriously considered. One of these was at the deposit stage. Nearly all of the schemes, adopted and proposed, were situated on former industrial land, mostly in urban areas.

The SPZ provisions apply to Great Britain. An SPZ, which once declared also lasts for ten years, provides a simplified planning framework similar to that in an enterprise zone, except that it applies to such development or classes of development specified in the scheme, as opposed to a general permission for all developments except those excluded. The financial benefits of an enterprise zone are not available in an SPZ, except that there are no fees to pay for planning applications. Unlike an enterprise zone, which is declared by the Government, an SPZ is introduced by the local planning authority concerned. The procedures for introducing an SPZ are broadly similar to those for a local plan.

Powers for the Government to streamline the procedure for adopting an SPZ were included in the Planning and Compensation Act 1991. The Government intends to do this by:

—streamlining pre-deposit publicity arrangements;

—speeding up the pre-adoption procedures; and

—limiting the requirement to hold a public inquiry to cases where important planning issues are raised.

The Government has consulted on the implementation of these proposals, and it is intended that the necessary regulations will come into force later in 1992.

Conservation Areas

Some areas receive special protection as 'conservation areas'. These are areas of special architectural or historic interest whose character or appearance is such that it is desirable that they should be preserved or enhanced. A conservation area can be designated by the local planning authority, which has a duty to consider whether there are any areas within its boundaries that deserve this protection. In order to designate a conservation area, the council has to advertise the proposal and hold a public meeting at which the plans can be discussed by local residents. The Secretary of State also has the power to designate a conservation area. There are over 7,000 conservation areas in England, more than 550 in Scotland, over 350 in Wales and 28 in Northern Ireland.

Once a conservation area has been designated, stricter planning rules apply. For example, some of the formerly permitted development rights are taken away, such as the demolition of buildings and the felling of trees. Any such development would now need planning permission. Planning applications that the local planning authority considers would affect the character of the area have to be advertised. Moreover, a stricter test is applied when applications are determined: the council has to pay special attention to the desirability of preserving or enhancing the character or appearance of the area. Demolition of houses within conservation areas is forbidden without conservation area consent, and the maximum penalties are considerable: up to 12 months' imprisonment and/or an unlimited fine.

Another form of protection for an area of special character can be given by means of an 'article 4 direction'. This is provided for in article 4 of the General Development Order, and has the effect of removing some or all permitted development rights from the properties concerned. Alterations specified in a direction, for example the addition of satellite dishes, sun porches, double glazing and vehicle driveways—normally permitted development but which insensitively done can harm the appearance of a street or area— would then require specific planning permission. This gives the local planning authority means to control such changes.

Normally an article 4 direction needs the approval of the Secretary of State, who has the right to make modifications, although a council can make a temporary six-month direction for certain sorts of development. Once a direction has been approved, the planning authority has to give notice of it, either by serving notice on all landholders in the affected area or, if this is impracticable, by means of a newspaper advertisement.

Listed Buildings and Ancient Monuments

Ancient monuments and important buildings are protected through the planning system. There are a considerable number of such sites and buildings in Britain. Buildings of historic or architectural importance are listed by one of three grades; Grade I (the most important), Grade II* and Grade II. The decision to list a building is made by the relevant Secretary of State[2] after taking advice from the heritage body concerned (in England, English Heritage). In addition, local planning authorities have the power to make a building preservation notice. This lasts for six months, and protects the building while the Secretary of State considers whether or not to make a permanent listing.

Once a building is listed, it enjoys a considerable degree of protection. Before alterations which would affect its character are made to it, listed building consent must be obtained from the local planning authority. Listed building consent is also required for its demolition. It is an offence to carry out these activities without getting this permission, and the penalties for non-compliance are severe (again, up to 12 months' imprisonment and an unlimited fine). A recent report from English Heritage showed that while most listed buildings are in reasonable condition, some 7 per cent are at risk from decay.

[2]In England, the Secretary of State for National Heritage.

Table 4: Scheduled Buildings

	Scheduled Monuments	Listed Buildings
England	13,000	440,000
Scotland	5,000	37,000
Wales	2,700	14,000
Northern Ireland	1,200	8,000

Sources: Department of the Environment, Scottish Office, Welsh Office, Department of the Environment for Northern Ireland.

The listed building control system operates in a manner similar to development control. The relevant Secretary of State[3] has responsibility for new legislation and for issuing guidance on policy matters. Listed building inquiries and appeals are dealt with by the Planning Inspectorate and the Secretary of State has powers to call in listed building consent applications and to decide appeals.

Applications for listed building consent are made to local planning authorities. Certain applications, particularly those affecting Grades I and II* buildings, have to be referred to the Secretary of State if the authority is minded to grant consent, to give him an opportunity to call in the application for his own decision. Similar appeal and enforcement systems apply to listed building applications as to applications for planning permission, but there are no fees for these applications.

To be eligible for scheduling, ancient monuments must be of national importance in accordance with agreed criteria. The decision on whether to schedule is taken by the relevant Secretary of State[4], in Great Britain after taking advice from English Heritage

[3]In England, the Secretary of State for the Environment.
[4]In England, the Secretary of State for National Heritage.

or its equivalent. Once a monument has been scheduled, any works to repair or alter it require scheduled monument consent in writing from the relevant Secretary of State. Government guidance stresses the need for developers to discuss their preliminary plans for development with the local planning authority at an early stage to ensure that the potential effect on archaeological remains can be assessed and taken into account in deciding whether to grant planning permission.

Green Belts

'Green Belts' are areas designated in development plans to be left open. They are intended to:

—check the unrestricted sprawl of large built-up areas;

—safeguard the surrounding countryside from further encroachment;

—prevent neighbouring towns from merging into one another;

—preserve the special character of historic towns; and

—assist in urban regeneration.

The first Green Belt was set up around London just before the second world war; in 1955 the Government decided to extend them to other locations. They have now been established around other major cities, including Edinburgh, Glasgow, Greater Manchester, Merseyside and the West Midlands. Green Belts have also been established around some smaller towns and cities, such as Oxford, Cambridge, Cheltenham and Gloucester, Derby and Nottingham, and York. Green Belts vary in size from the largest, of 4,800 sq km (1,900 sq miles) around London to the smallest, of just 7 sq km (3 sq miles) around Burton-on-Trent in Staffordshire.

In all, some 1.5 million hectares (3.8 million acres) are designated as Green Belt in England, and 145,000 hectares (360,000
acres) in Scotland. There has been a very considerable increase in
the total area of land designated as Green Belt in recent years. Over
the period 1979–89, the area of Green Belt in England more than
doubled.

Table 5: Green Belt by Region 1979–89

		Sq km
	1979	1x989
Northern	400	504
Yorkshire & Humberside	1,263	2,480
East Midlands	–	615
Eastern	17	108
South East	3,319	6,052
South West	685	818
West Midlands	1,425	2,458
North West	15	2,451
Scotland	2,185	1,446

Sources: Department of the Environment, Scottish Office.

The Government attaches great importance to the protection of
Green Belts and expects local planning authorities to do likewise
when considering planning applications. Apart from a limited
range of developments appropriate for a rural area, permission for
new buildings or changes of use should only be given in exceptional circumstances. The Government's commitment to Green Belts
was re-affirmed in the White Paper *This Common Inheritance*,
which pointed out that 58 per cent of new housing in the South
East was being built on re-used land—thus fulfilling one of the

aims of Green Belt policy. The designation of Green Belts is a matter for the local planning authorities drawing up the development plans for the areas concerned. The Government can use its powers in the making of plans to ensure that sufficient attention is paid to the importance of Green Belts. For example, the Government intervened in July 1990 to halt plans to reduce greatly the area of Green Belt around Chester. The Government subsequently put forward modifications to the plan which would maintain the general extent of the Green Belt.

There are no Green Belts in Wales. However, at the request of the Secretary of State for Wales, the Assembly of Welsh Counties is currently co-ordinating an assessment of the potential contribution of statutory Green Belts to the proper planning and development of Wales.

Hazardous Substances

The Planning (Hazardous Substances) Act 1990 came into force in June 1992. This enables local authorities to decide whether the presence of a significant quantity of a hazardous substance is appropriate in a particular location, having regard to existing and prospective development in the vicinity. The controls are concerned with the storage and use of substances which could present a major fire, explosion or toxic hazard to people in the surrounding area. Hazardous substances consent is required where a named hazardous substance is to be present at or above a specified amount, known as the 'controlled quantity'.

Although local planning authorities had hitherto been able to exercise a degree of control over the siting and use of hazardous substances, where a planning application was made to them involving the use of hazardous substances, such substances may be introduced onto a site without any development being involved. The new provisions thus enable control to be exercised in circumstances other than where development requiring planning permission is proposed. The controls do not override or duplicate health and safety legislation; they deal with the residual risk that remains after health and safety requirements have been complied with.

Development in the Countryside

New government guidance on the countryside and the rural economy was published in January 1992. This emphasises that, while development is necessary to sustain the rural economy, it must be balanced with protection of the countryside. Other points covered in the new guidance include:

—a presumption against major new developments in the National Parks, except in exceptional circumstances where such development would be in the public interest;

—an emphasis on new directions and opportunities in the countryside as employment in traditional industries declines; and

—advice on the operation of new stricter planning controls over the siting and design of agricultural buildings.

At the same time as the new guidance, there were some significant changes to the planning regime as it affects farmers, stemming from the need to ensure that new buildings respect the landscape and natural environment. On farms of 5 hectares or more, planning regulations now give local planning authorities control over the siting, design and external appearance of some new agricultural buildings and significant extensions erected under permitted development rights—powers previously enjoyed only by National Park authorities. On smaller farms (those between 0.4 and 5 hectares), planning permission is required for these developments. The construction of new dwellings in the countryside remains subject to planning permission.

Sport and the Countryside

New guidance on sport and leisure was published in September 1991. This emphasised the protection of the countryside for leisure uses. It recognised the growing demand for golf courses, but stressed that these should be designed to be in harmony with the surrounding countryside and to conserve the natural environment. Associated developments, such as hotels, should be considered on their own merits. It also stressed the need to protect open spaces in urban areas for recreation and amenity purposes.

National Parks and Areas of Outstanding Natural Beauty

Areas of great landscape importance in England and Wales can be designated National Parks, of which there are currently ten covering a total of 13,600 sq km (5,300 sq miles). National Parks are designated by the Countryside Commission (in England) or the Countryside Council for Wales, subject to confirmation by the respective Secretaries of State. The criteria for designation of these extensive tracts of countryside are the desirability to conserve and enhance the natural beauty of the area and to promote its enjoyment by the public. They are national in the sense that they are of value to the nation as a whole; most of the land within them remains in private hands. Each National Park has its own authority, funded partly by the Government and partly by the county councils concerned. In addition, the Norfolk and Suffolk Broads Authority was created in 1989 to give the area status and protection similar to a National Park. It was announced in January 1992 that steps would be taken to designate the New Forest an area of national significance. The Government has also announced proposals to establish independent National Park authorities and to ensure local representation on them.

Within a National Park, the National Park authority is the local planning authority and is responsible for the preparation of a local plan covering the whole Park. Within a National Park, people do not enjoy the same scope to carry out permitted developments; instead a number of alterations that would be free of control elsewhere, such as the installation of dormer windows, require planning permission.

The Countryside Commission and the Countryside Council for Wales can also designate areas of important landscape quality as Areas of Outstanding Natural Beauty (AONBs), subject to the confirmation of the relevant Secretary of State. A total of 39 AONBs have been declared in England and Wales, covering a total of 20,400 sq km (7,960 sq miles). The primary objective of designation is the conservation of the natural beauty of the landscape; local authorities are encouraged to give special attention to AONBs in their planning and countryside conservation work. As in National Parks, the rules on permitted development are more restrictive in AONBs than they are elsewhere.

In Scotland, there are no National Parks, but four regional parks and 40 National Scenic Areas have been created, covering more than 1 million hectares (2.5 million acres). Within these areas, certain kinds of development can be carried out only after consultation with Scottish Natural Heritage, the Scottish nature conservation and countryside body. In the event of a disagreement, the Secretary of State for Scotland can be consulted. In Northern

Ireland, nine AONBs have been declared, covering an area of 282,000 hectares (698,000 acres).

Conservation of Natural Heritage

Sites that are important to Britain's natural heritage are protected by statutory notification as Sites of Special Scientific Interest (SSSIs) or, in Northern Ireland, Areas of Special Scientific Interest (ASSIs). In March 1991 there were some 5,670 SSSIs and 36 ASSIs in Britain. Some SSSIs are of international importance, and as such have been designated under the European Community directive on wild birds as Special Protection Areas, of which there were 47 in April 1992. Similarly, 53 sites have been designated for protection under the Ramsar Convention on wetlands of international importance. The proposed European Community directive on habitats, which is aimed at ensuring the maintenance of threatened species and habitats throughout the Community, will introduce Special Areas of Conservation. It is expected that a comprehensive network of protected areas will be established by the year 2000.[5]

The Government has provided additional protection for SSSIs in England and Wales from January 1992. For instance, permitted development rights for temporary recreational uses such as motor sports and clay pigeon shooting on SSSIs were withdrawn, and there is now a legal requirement for local planning authorities to consult the appropriate government nature conservation bodies (either English Nature or the Countryside Council for Wales) about planning applications adjacent to SSSIs; such consultation was already necessary for applications directly on SSSIs.

[5]For more information on the protection of Britain's natural heritage, see the companion title *Conservation*, currently in preparation.

Councils' Own Development

Councils often make developments of their own—new schools, offices or leisure centres, for example. In these cases, the council is not exempt from the requirements of the planning system. It therefore has to apply for planning permission for its developments, even though that may mean applying to itself.

In cases where the council has to apply to itself for permission, its role as a local planning authority is quite distinct from the role in which it applies for such permission. The application has to be treated in accordance with certain procedures, in order to ensure public confidence in the handling of the process. In August 1991, the Government announced proposals for new regulations to handle authorities' own developments. These would stipulate that:

—local planning authorities would be able to grant themselves permission, but where the proposal was for another party to develop their land, the application must be determined by the relevant development control authority;[6]

—councils would not be able to use the confidentiality provisions of the Local Government Act 1972 to discuss their own development proposals in meetings closed to the general public;

—planning permission granted for authorities' own development would not pass to subsequent owners of the land, unlike normal practice; and

—applications would not be determined by a committee or officer also responsible for the management of the land or building concerned.

New regulations were introduced in July 1992.

[6]Thus, for example, a county council could grant itself permission to build a school, but if it wanted to sell a school playing field with permission for housing, it would have to seek planning permission from the district council.

Tree and Hedgerow Protection

Local planning authorities have a duty to ensure that when grant-ing planning permission they make adequate provision for preser-vation and planting of trees by imposing conditions. They also have powers to protect trees or areas of woodland by means of Tree Preservation Orders (TPOs). Once a local planning authority has placed a TPO on a tree, it is an offence to fell or lop it without their permission, with exceptions such as the felling of dead or danger-ous trees. Where permission is given to fell a protected tree, the landowner can be required to plant a replacement. It is a criminal offence to act in contravention of a TPO. In conservation areas, a landowner must give notice to the local planning authority when he intends to carry out felling or works on a tree; until expiry of the notification period, the tree is protected as if covered by a TPO.

In *This Common Inheritance*, the Government said that it would introduce measures to safeguard key hedgerows. Following a consultation paper, it has announced plans to:

—require owners and occupiers of land to give prior notice to local planning authorities of proposed hedgerow removal; and

—give local authorities powers to register such hedgerows, where appropriate, to ensure their retention.

A separate scheme provides incentives to promote the improved management of hedgerows in ways which are environmentally ben-eficial.

Strategic Views Across London

Protection has long been given through the planning system to the so-called 'strategic views across London': long-distance views of two of the capital's principal monuments, the Palace of Westminster and, especially, St Paul's Cathedral.

The Government has issued guidance requiring boroughs in London to incorporate into their UDPs protection to eight views of St Paul's and two of the Palace of Westminster from important points, usually high ground. Examples of such protected views include the view from Primrose Hill to both sites, and from Kenwood to St Paul's. Developments which would spoil these views should be refused. This does not prevent councils from also deciding to protect other views.

Strategic Issues and Future Directions

Britain's planning system has evolved and altered to cope with new pressures and situations.

Regional Planning

Although Britain's population has increased only slowly, the number of households has been rising in recent years, and is projected to increase further in the period to 2011. Moreover, this increase will not be uniform across the country as a whole, but will be especially strong in certain regions, and less marked in others.

Table 6: Projected Number of Households, England

	1991 (000s)	2011 (000s)	Growth (per cent)
East Anglia	821	1,029	25
South West	1,882	2,295	22
East Midlands	1,602	1,931	21
South East	7,000	8,072	15
Yorkshire and Humberside	1,982	2,234	13
West Midlands	2,045	2,289	12
North West	2,493	2,707	9
North	1,210	1,295	7

Source: Department of the Environment

The disparity between the population growth of the different regions will lead to different needs and pressures with which the planning system will have to deal. For example, in March 1991 the Government set out its priorities for determining the location of development within and beyond the South East:

— the protection of the environment in the South East where it is under threat from excessive development;

— the stimulation of development in those parts of the country where it is most needed, especially by means of regenerating older towns and cities and re-using derelict and under-utilised land; and

— the development of those less-prosperous parts of the South East which have potential for accommodating growth.

Similarly, in regional guidance for East Anglia, published in July 1991, the Government encourages environmentally sustainable growth and the dispersal of investment and jobs to the less prosperous parts of the region. This need to direct investment to less prosperous areas is despite the rapid growth in East Anglia as a whole in recent years.

A special study is being conducted on the potential of the East Thames Corridor for development and environmental enhancement. In November 1991 consultants were appointed to examine the development capacity of the lower Thames—the area extending eastwards from the London Docklands to Tilbury in Essex and Sheerness in Kent. Serplan had proposed this area as a possible future location for growth within the South East region. The area contains a number of large development sites close to the route which has been adopted for the high speed rail link between London and the continent of Europe via the Channel Tunnel. The consultants were asked to make an appraisal not only of the potential for development and the transport and other infrastructure needs but also the scope for improving the environment and for protecting and enhancing ecologically sensitive sites.

Land for Housing

The increase in households is creating a need for new housing, especially in regions where much of the population growth is occurring. The pressure that this causes is strong in the South East, where much of the land around existing cities is designated as Green Belt. Developers have been calling for sufficient land to be made available to meet future housing needs. Planning applications for new homes, however, have often been opposed strongly by people already living in the vicinity. Other problems have occurred in rural areas, where many homes have been bought by town-dwellers, thus putting considerable pressure on the existing population. Regional guidance from the Government sets out the number of new homes that development plans should make provision for. Government guidance now states that rural land may exceptionally be released for affordable housing, provided that there are safeguards to ensure that the housing continues to meet the needs of local people.

The present regional guidance for the South East, published in February 1989, suggests that the following numbers of new homes are needed in the region between 1991 and 2001:

Bedfordshire	20,000	Hertfordshire	34,500
Berkshire	29,500	Isle of Wight	5,000
Buckinghamshire	32,000	Kent	55,000
East Sussex	22,000	Oxfordshire	23,000
Essex	53,000	Surrey	26,000
Greater London	175,000	West Sussex	28,000
Hampshire	66,500		

Research commissioned by the Government and published in January 1991 suggested that over the period between 1981 and 2001 less than 1 per cent of rural land in England was likely to change to urban use. The Government believes that the need for new housing can be met to a considerable extent from the re-use of existing sites. In the South East, for example, about half of new housebuilding in recent years has taken place on derelict land or in urban areas rather than on greenfield sites. Indeed, the encouragement of urban regeneration is one of the explicit aims of the Green Belt system. Moreover, many of the additional households are made up of elderly or single people whose housing needs may be better met within towns and by the conversion of existing large buildings into smaller units.

New Settlements

However, some building on new sites will continue to be needed. One solution that has been put forward to accommodate the need for new housing while at the same time avoiding the sprawl of existing towns and cities is the creation of new settlements. These would be small towns or villages built by private-sector developers, differing from the Government's postwar New Town programme by the size of the settlements envisaged, and without recourse to special administrative structures such as new town development corporations.

A number of new settlements, ranging from small villages to small towns, have been proposed in recent years. Examples have included:

—Northwick, a proposal for a settlement of 4,000 houses and associated business and community facilities on Canvey Island (Essex);

—Great Lea, a proposal for up to 3,200 homes and a shopping centre south of Reading in Berkshire; and

—Foxley Wood, a proposal for 4,800 houses in Hampshire.

Many of the settlement proposals have been unpopular with local people. All the above examples were refused planning permission.

In the light of recent experiences, the Government has issued fresh advice on new settlements. This does not reject the concept of new settlements, but to be successful a proposal for a new settlement would normally have to meet a number of requirements, that:

—the alternative of expanding existing towns or villages would represent a less satisfactory way of providing land for the new housing that is needed;

—the proposal is a clear expression of local preferences supported by local planning authorities;

—the proposed new settlement would present no risk of unacceptable coalescence with existing settlements;

—the option of a new settlement, in preference to the alternative, would result in positive environmental improvements, for example through reclamation of derelict land, or upgrading of areas of low landscape value;

—the proposal can be considered alongside policies of restraint to protect the rejected alternative locations from development pressure; and

—it is not within a Green Belt, National Park, AONB, SSSI or on the best or most versatile agricultural land.

In this way the Government hopes that the net effect of a new settlement will either enhance the environment or cause only modest environmental impact which would be outweighed by the need to meet housing requirements. The guidance says that the need to respect local preference means that specific proposals for new settlements should normally only be promoted through the district-wide local plan or UDP.

Affordable Housing

The Government has issued guidance on affordable housing. This encourages local planning authorities to take the need for affordable housing into account when formulating their development plans and making planning decisions. The guidance encourages planning authorities to negotiate with developers to include a proportion of affordable housing in new housebuilding schemes, according to local site and market conditions. Development plans should also include policies announcing their intention of so doing, and include the criteria to be used to assess whether a particular proposal meets the objectives of the policy, although the guidance warns against making general quotas for such housing.

Environmental Matters

As awareness of environmental matters has grown, so the planning system has increasingly had to take into account the demands of meeting environmental standards. Local planning authorities are now required to take environmental considerations into account when formulating development plans, in particular by consulting with the major national conservation agencies before putting their plans on deposit.

In order to combat the threat of climate change, the Government is laying increased stress on the use of renewable energy, having undertaken in *This Common Inheritance* to work towards the installation of new renewable generating capacity of

1,000 megawatts by the year 2000. New draft guidance for England and Wales on renewable energy installations such as wind farms and water turbines was issued for consultation in December 1991. This shows how local planning authorities can include renewable energy policies in development plans and sets out the considerations that should apply when renewable energy installations are proposed in designated areas. Information is also given on the assessment of the environmental impact of wind-powered developments, and further annexes on other forms of renewable energy will be issued.

Technological Changes

The introduction of new technology into many walks of life could have an impact on the planning system. For example, the development of satellite communications, especially television, has meant that planning rules on satellite dishes needed to be devised.

The rules on the placement of satellite television dishes on people's houses is an example of how the planning system can be adjusted to take account of changed circumstances. Regulations had been introduced to control the spread of dishes, which insensitively done can have a bad effect on a neighbourhood's appearance. These rules allowed one dish per house to be installed as permitted development, provided that it was not larger than 90 cm in diameter and that it was not mounted above the roofline. In November 1990, however, the Government proposed to alter this to allow two dishes per house, since there were at that time two separate channels. The merger of these two channels made that unnecessary. When new regulations were introduced in July 1991, therefore, the one-dish limit for permitted development remained, but the size of the dish was limited to 70 cm, most of the popular dishes being around 60 cm in diameter. The Government has also published guidelines for householders to explain these regulations.

As a further example, the growth in telecommunications generally, and mobile telephones in particular, has created a need for many new facilities—for example antennae for cellular telephones on many buildings. Currently the operators of such equipment enjoy significant permitted development rights, subject to restrictions on height and size to protect the environment. However, the telecommunications industry has advanced rapidly since these rights were introduced in 1985, and local planning authorities have accumulated considerable experience of implementing the present system. The Government has therefore instituted a review of planning controls over such apparatus.

Addresses

Department of the Environment, 2 Marsham Street, London SW1P 3EB.

Department of the Environment for Northern Ireland, Parliament Buildings, Stormont, Belfast BT4 3SS.

Scottish Office, St Andrew's House, Edinburgh EH1 3DE.

Welsh Office, Cathays Park, Cardiff CF1 3NQ.

English Heritage, Fortress House, 23 Savile Row, London W1X 1AB.

Planning Inspectorate, Tollgate House, Houlton Street, Bristol BS2 9DJ.

Further Reading

£

This Common Inheritance.
Cm 1200. ISBN 0 10 112002 8.   HMSO   1990   27.00

This Common Inheritance:
the First Year Report.
Cm 1655. ISBN 0 10 116552 8.   HMSO   1991   21.00

Enforcing Planning Control
(the Carnwath Report).
ISBN 0 11 752194 9   HMSO   1989   8.00

The Green Belts.
Department of the Environment.
ISBN 0 11 752143 4   HMSO   1988   4.95

Town and Country Planning
General Development Order.
ISBN 0 11 087813 2   HMSO   1988   6.80

Town and Country Planning Act 1990

Planning (Hazardous Substances) Act 1990

Planning (Listed Buildings and Conservation Areas) Act 1990

Planning (Consequential Provisions) Act 1990

Planning and Compensation Act 1991

Planning Policy Guidance Notes £

PPG 1   *General Policy and Principles.*
ISBN 0 11 752630 4   HMSO   1992   2.75

PPG 2   *Green Belts.*
ISBN 0 11 752054 3   HMSO   1988   1.10

PPG 3   *Housing.*
ISBN 0 11 752628 2   HMSO   1992   3.45

PPG 4   *Industrial and Commercial
Development and Small Firms.*
ISBN 0 11 752055 1   HMSO   1988   0.85

PPG 5   *Simplified Planning Zones.*
ISBN 0 11 752056 X   HMSO   1988   2.30

PPG 6   *Major Retail Development.*
ISBN 0 11 752069 1   HMSO   1988   1.70

PPG 7   *The Countryside and the
Rural Economy.*
ISBN 0 11 752585 5   HMSO   1992   5.20

PPG 8   *Telecommunications.*
ISBN 0 11 752057 8   HMSO   1988   3.10

PPG 9   *Regional Guidance for
the South East.*
ISBN 0 11 752190 6   HMSO   1989   2.30

PPG 10   *Strategic Guidance for
the West Midlands.*
ISBN 0 11 752136 1   HMSO   1988   1.70

PPG 11   *Strategic Guidance for Merseyside.*
ISBN 0 11 752149 3   HMSO   1988   1.70

£

PPG 12	Development Plans and Regional Planning Guidance. ISBN 0 11 752586 3	HMSO	1992	8.00
PPG 13	Highways Considerations in Development Control. ISBN 0 11 752155 8	HMSO	1988	2.40
PPG 14	Development on Unstable Land. ISBN 0 11 752300 3	HMSO	1990	3.50
PPG 16	Archaeology and Planning. ISBN 0 11 752353 4	HMSO	1990	4.30
PPG 18	Enforcing Planning Control. ISBN 0 11 752554 5	HMSO	1991	1.80
PPG 19	Outdoor Advertisement Control. ISBN 0 11 752555 3	HMSO	1992	1.95

Annual Reports

Chief Planning Inspector's Report April 1990 to March 1991.
ISBN 0 11 752548 0   HMSO   4.55

Written by Reference Services,
Central Office of Information.

Printed in the United Kingdom for HMSO.
Dd 0294541 C30 10/92